Complete Steps on How to Hatch and Care for Tilapia Fishes for Profits

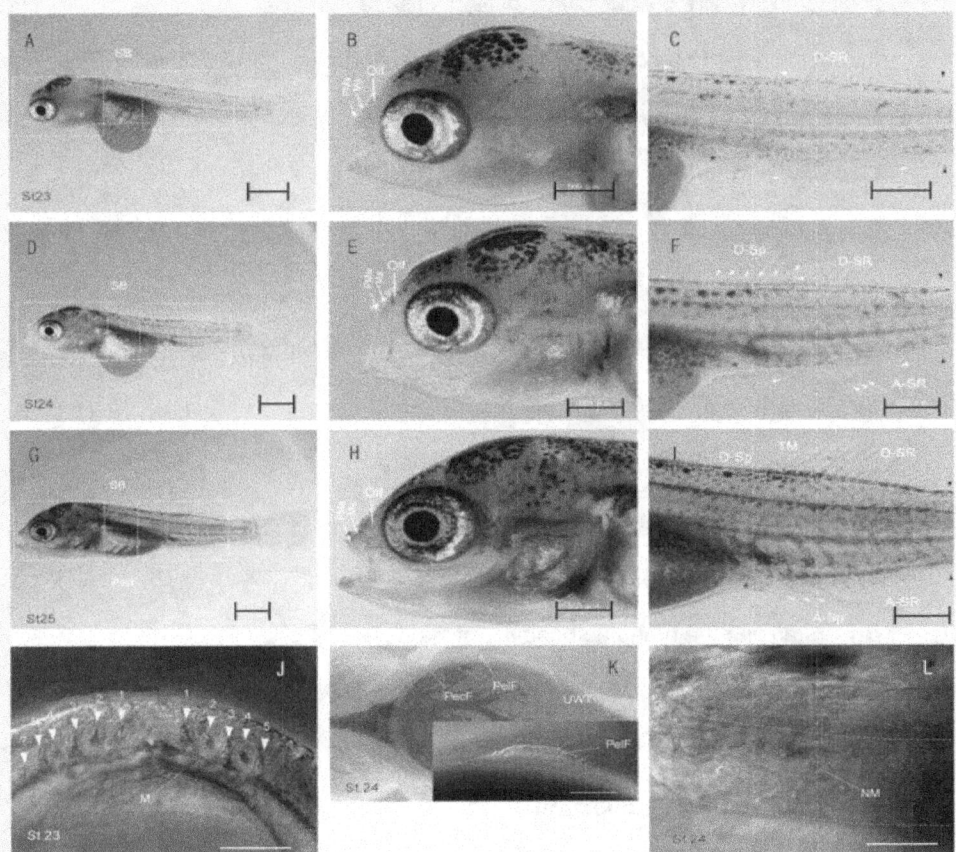

By

Benadine Nonye Nduagu

(www.Agric4profits.com)

Table of Contents

Chapter One

Introduction

This book covers every crucial aspect of the hatching and rearing process, providing readers with a thorough understanding of the necessary steps and considerations for successful tilapia fish farming.

Aquaculture, the practice of rearing fish and aquatic plants, has become an essential component of global food production. Among the various species cultivated in aquaculture, tilapia fish have gained significant attention for their adaptability, fast growth rate, and high nutritional value. Understanding the process of hatching tilapia fishes is crucial for anyone considering venturing into aquaculture, as it forms the foundation of successful fish farming.

1.1   Significance of Tilapia Fish Farming

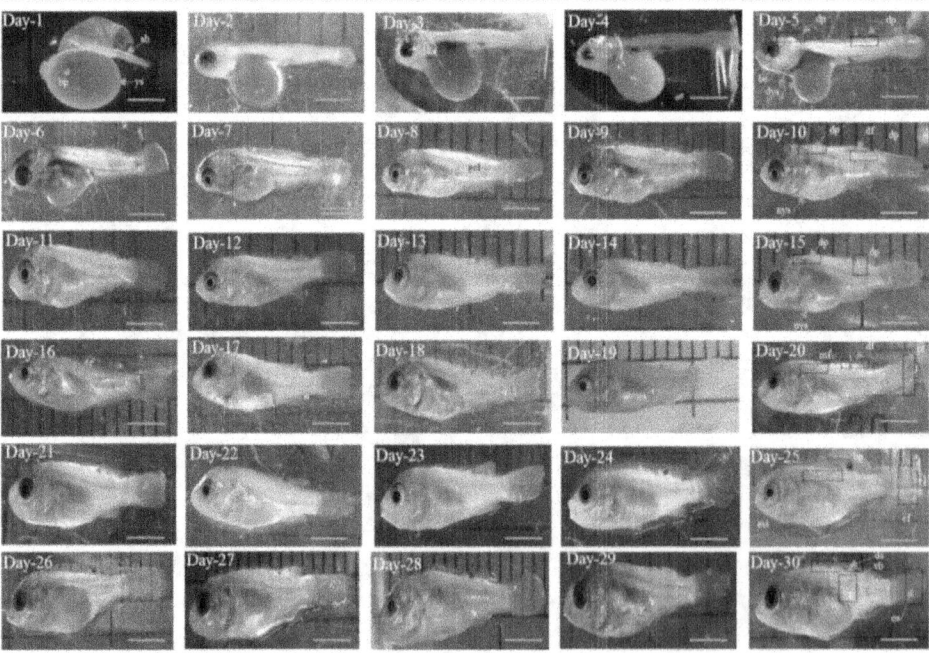

Tilapia fish, known for their resilience and versatility, have emerged as a popular choice for fish farming across the globe.

With their ability to thrive in diverse environmental conditions and their rapid growth rate, tilapia fish are an excellent option for both small-scale and large-scale aquaculture operations.

Furthermore, their high protein content and low levels of saturated fats make them a sought-after choice for health-conscious consumers.

1.2   The Importance of Hatching

The hatching process serves as the initial stage in tilapia fish farming, laying the groundwork for successful cultivation.

Understanding the intricacies of hatching is essential for ensuring the healthy development of the fish and achieving optimal growth rates.

This eBook will guide you through the comprehensive steps involved in the hatching process, from setting up the hatchery to the final stages of growth and harvest.

Through the following chapters, we will delve into the intricacies of tilapia fish breeding, the essentials of creating an ideal hatchery environment, effective egg collection and incubation techniques, and the intricacies of managing the growth stages of tilapia fish, including disease prevention and management.

By the end of this guide, you will have a thorough understanding of the entire hatching process, empowering you to embark on a successful tilapia fish farming journey.

Chapter Two

Understanding Tilapia Fish

Tilapia fish, belonging to the Cichlidae family, are a diverse group of freshwater fish that are widely cultivated for their adaptability and rapid growth.

Understanding the fundamental characteristics and behavior of tilapia fish is essential for successfully hatching and cultivating these aquatic species.

2.1   Overview of Tilapia Fish Species

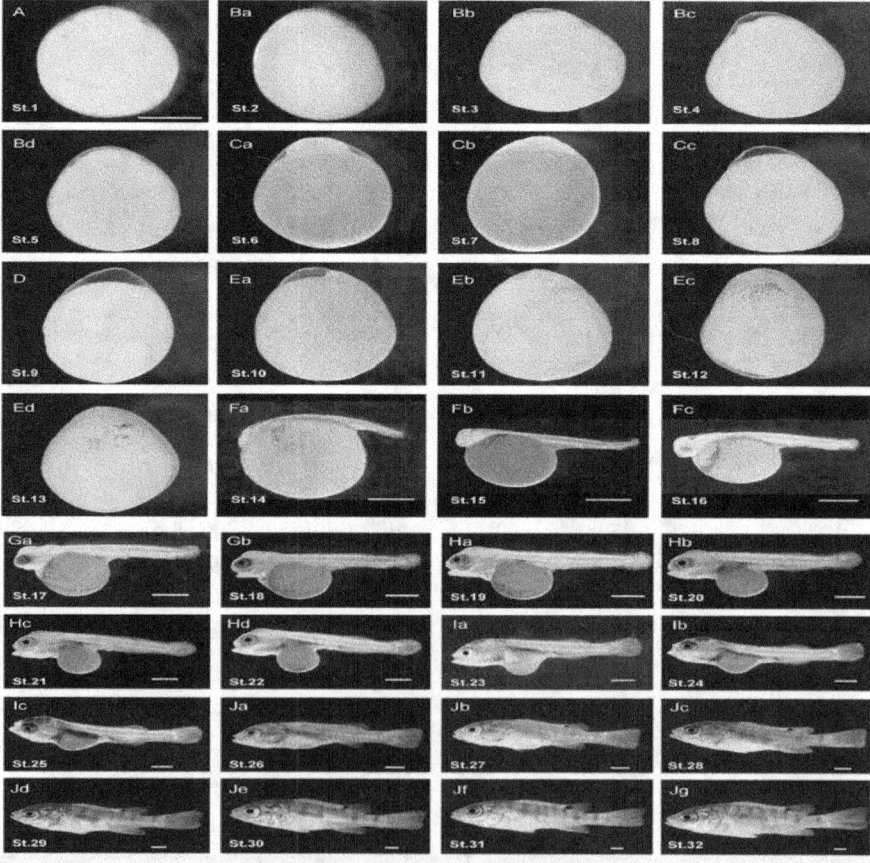

Tilapia fish encompass various species, with some of the most commonly farmed ones being Nile tilapia (Oreochromis niloticus), Mozambique tilapia (Oreochromis mossambicus), and blue tilapia (Oreochromis aureus).

Each species has its distinct characteristics, preferred environmental conditions, and growth patterns, which should be considered when planning a tilapia fish farming venture.

2.2 Characteristics and Behavior of Tilapia Fish

Tilapia fish are known for their tolerance to a wide range of environmental conditions, making them suitable for farming in various regions across the globe.

They are generally herbivorous, although some species can also exhibit omnivorous feeding behavior.

Understanding their dietary preferences and feeding habits is crucial for providing adequate nutrition during the different stages of their growth.

2.3 Importance of Tilapia Fish in Aquaculture

The popularity of tilapia fish in aquaculture stems from their rapid growth rate, high reproductive capacity, and resilience to fluctuating environmental conditions.

Moreover, their mild taste and firm texture make them a favored choice in the culinary world. As a result, tilapia fish farming has become an essential component of sustainable aquaculture practices, contributing significantly to global food security and economic development.

Understanding the intricacies of tilapia fish biology and behavior is crucial for ensuring their successful hatching and subsequent growth stages.

In the following sections, we will delve into the step-by-step process of setting up an effective hatchery and the techniques involved in tilapia fish breeding and spawning, laying the foundation for a successful tilapia fish farming operation.

Chapter Three

Setting Up the Hatchery

Establishing a well-designed and properly equipped hatchery is crucial for ensuring the successful hatching and initial stages of growth for tilapia fish.

An efficiently organized hatchery provides the optimal conditions necessary for the eggs and larvae to develop and thrive.

This section will guide you through the essential steps in setting up an effective tilapia fish hatchery.

3.1   Selecting the Right Location for the Hatchery

Choosing an appropriate location for the tilapia fish hatchery is a critical first step.

The site should have access to a consistent and reliable water supply, be protected from environmental disturbances, and offer sufficient space for the hatchery infrastructure.

Additionally, it should be easily accessible for routine maintenance and monitoring.

3.2 Designing and Constructing the Tilapia Hatchery

The design of the hatchery should incorporate the necessary components to facilitate the hatching and rearing processes.

This includes the construction of suitable tanks or ponds, the installation of aeration systems to maintain water quality, and the implementation of a reliable filtration system to remove waste and maintain optimal conditions for the fish.

3.3 Water Quality Requirements for the Hatchery

Maintaining high water quality is imperative for the successful hatching and rearing of tilapia fish.

The water temperature, pH levels, dissolved oxygen content, and ammonia concentrations should be carefully monitored and regulated to create a favorable environment for the eggs and larvae.

Implementing regular water quality testing and ensuring effective management practices are essential for the health and development of the fish.

A well-planned and properly equipped hatchery lays the foundation for successful tilapia fish farming.

The following sections will delve into the intricacies of tilapia fish breeding, the techniques for inducing spawning, and the crucial aspects of monitoring the spawning process.

Understanding these critical steps is vital for ensuring the successful hatching and growth of healthy tilapia fish.

Chapter Four

Breeding and Spawning

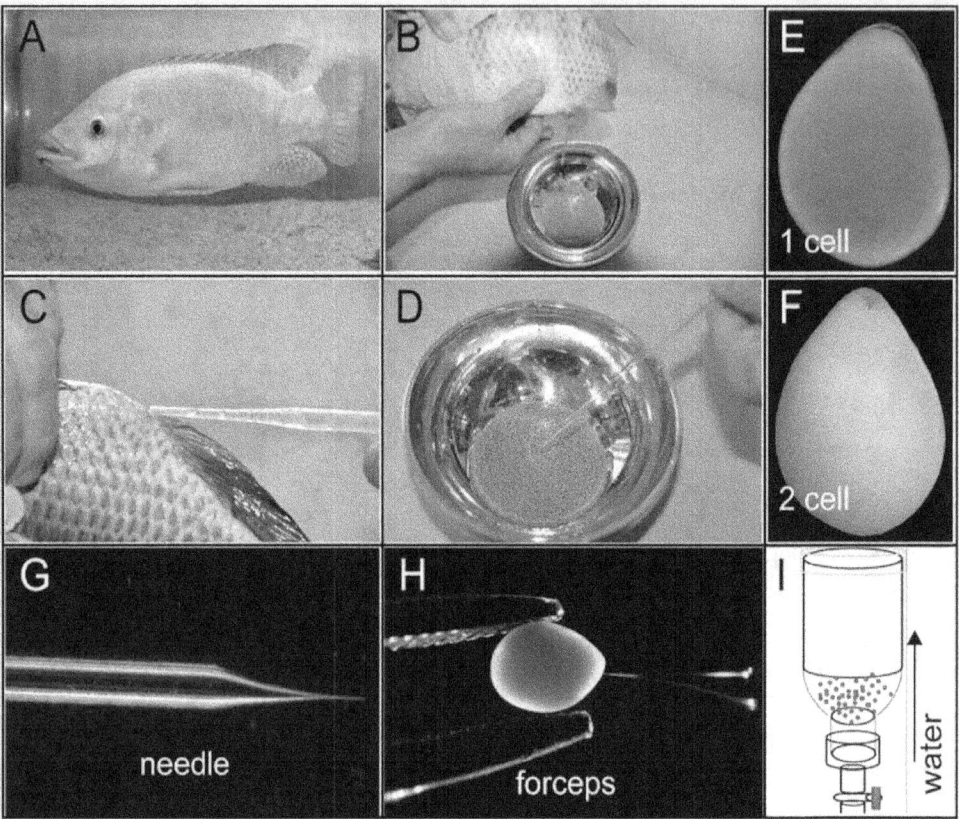

Understanding the intricacies of tilapia fish breeding and spawning is crucial for the successful propagation of these aquatic species.

Effective breeding techniques and careful monitoring of the spawning process are essential for ensuring the production of a healthy and robust offspring.

Consider the following key steps in the breeding and spawning process for tilapia fish.

4.1   Understanding the Breeding Behavior of Tilapia Fish

Tilapia fish exhibit various mating behaviors, including courtship rituals and territorial displays. Understanding their breeding behavior is essential for creating an environment conducive to successful reproduction.

Factors such as the male-to-female ratio, age and size of the breeding stock, and environmental conditions play a critical role in the breeding process.

4.2   Techniques for Inducing Spawning in Tilapia

Inducing spawning in tilapia fish often requires the manipulation of environmental conditions, such as temperature and light cycles.

Hormonal treatments may also be employed to stimulate the spawning process. Implementing effective spawning induction techniques is crucial for synchronizing the reproductive cycles of the fish and maximizing the yield of viable eggs.

4.3   Monitoring the Spawning Process

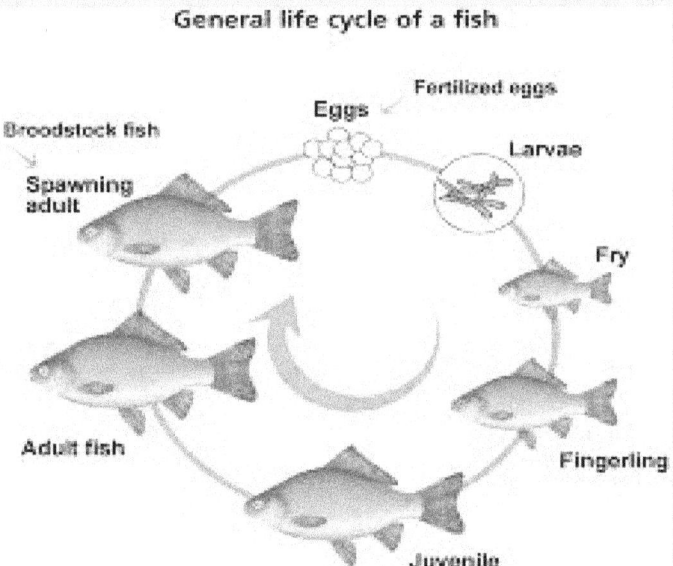

Close monitoring of the spawning process is essential for ensuring the successful fertilization of the eggs.

Regular observation of the breeding pairs, collection of fertilized eggs, and removal of unfertilized eggs are critical steps in the spawning process.

Maintaining optimal water quality and environmental conditions during this phase is vital for the healthy development of the embryos.

A thorough understanding of the intricacies of tilapia fish breeding and spawning is essential for ensuring successful egg production and subsequent hatching.

In the following sections, we will explore effective techniques for egg collection and incubation, laying the foundation for the healthy development of tilapia fish larvae in the hatchery.

Chapter Five

Egg Collection and Incubation

The process of collecting tilapia fish eggs and ensuring their successful incubation is a critical phase in the hatching process.

Implementing effective techniques for egg collection and providing optimal incubation conditions are essential for the healthy development of tilapia fish embryos. Consider the following key steps in the egg collection and incubation process.

5.1   Strategies for Collecting Tilapia Fish Eggs

Tilapia fish eggs are typically collected immediately after spawning to ensure their viability.

Gentle handling of the eggs and careful extraction from the breeding tanks are essential to prevent damage or contamination.

Utilizing specialized tools and equipment designed for egg collection can help maintain the integrity of the eggs and maximize their hatchability.

5.2   Creating the Ideal Conditions for Egg Incubation

Maintaining optimal environmental conditions during the incubation phase is crucial for the successful development of tilapia fish embryos.

Factors such as water temperature, oxygen levels, and water flow should be carefully regulated to promote proper embryonic development.

Implementing reliable incubation systems, such as hatchery trays or specialized incubation tanks, can provide a stable environment for the eggs to hatch.

5.3 Monitoring the Incubation Process and Addressing Challenges

Regular monitoring of the incubation process is essential for identifying any potential issues or challenges that may arise.

Ensuring the cleanliness of the incubation tanks, monitoring water quality parameters, and observing the developmental progress of the embryos are critical steps in the incubation phase.

Prompt identification and mitigation of any challenges can significantly improve the hatchability and survival rate of the tilapia fish larvae.

By implementing effective egg collection techniques and providing optimal incubation conditions, you can significantly increase the success rate of tilapia fish hatching.

In the following sections, we will look into the intricacies of larval rearing and the essential strategies for managing the growth stages of tilapia fish, setting the stage for their successful transition to the grow-out phase.

Chapter Six

Larval Rearing

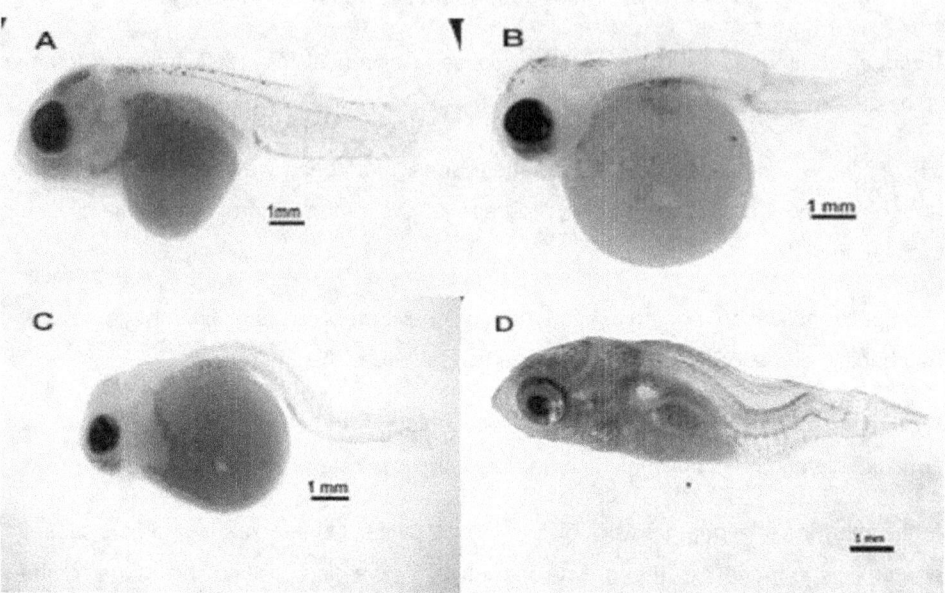

The larval rearing phase is a crucial stage in the hatching process of tilapia fish, as it sets the foundation for their subsequent growth and development.

Providing appropriate nutrition, maintaining optimal water quality, and preventing the onset of diseases are essential for ensuring the healthy growth of tilapia fish larvae. Consider the following key steps in the larval rearing process.

6.1 Feeding Techniques for Tilapia Fish Larvae

Tilapia fish larvae have specific nutritional requirements that must be met to promote healthy growth and development.

Implementing appropriate feeding techniques, such as providing specialized larval feed and maintaining a regular feeding schedule, is essential for ensuring the optimal nutrition of the larvae.

Monitoring the feeding behavior and adjusting the feeding regimen accordingly can help prevent malnutrition and promote robust growth.

6.2   Water Quality Management During the Larval Rearing Stage

Maintaining optimal water quality is critical for the healthy development of tilapia fish larvae.

Factors such as water temperature, dissolved oxygen levels, and ammonia concentration should be closely monitored and regulated to prevent stress and disease outbreaks.

Implementing effective water filtration systems and regular water quality testing can help create a conducive environment for the larvae to thrive.

6.3   Preventing Diseases and Maintaining Health

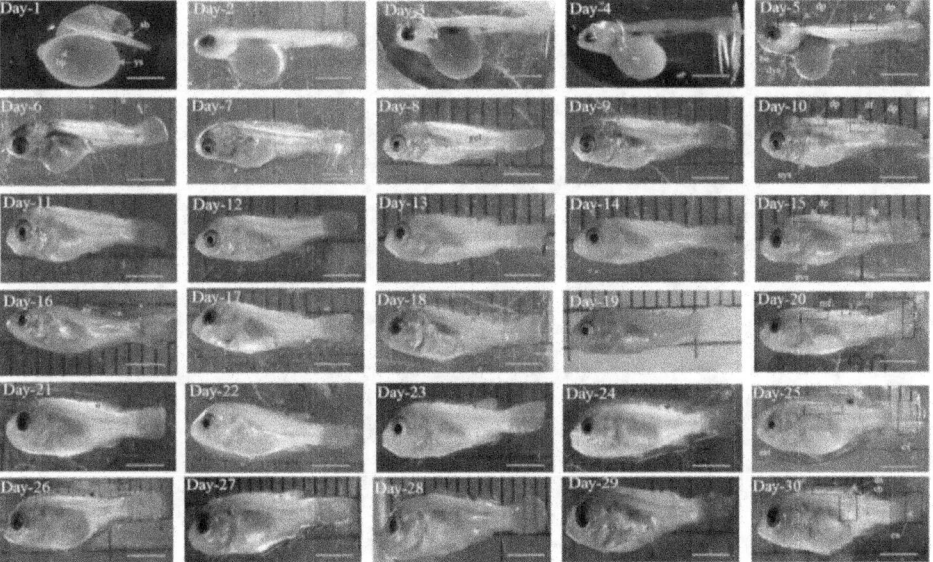

Tilapia fish larvae are susceptible to various diseases and infections, which can significantly impact their growth and survival rates.

Implementing strict biosecurity measures, practicing proper hygiene protocols, and regularly monitoring the health of the larvae are essential for preventing the onset of diseases.

Prompt identification of any signs of illness and the timely implementation of appropriate treatment measures can significantly improve the overall health and well-being of the tilapia fish larvae.

By prioritizing appropriate feeding techniques, maintaining optimal water quality, and implementing effective disease prevention strategies, you can ensure the successful rearing of tilapia fish larvae.

In the following sections, we will explore the essential strategies for managing the growth stages of tilapia fish and ensuring their successful transition to the grow-out phase.

Chapter Seven

Fry Management and Growth

© Aller Aqua Research

Managing the growth stages of tilapia fish fry is a critical phase in the hatching process, as it sets the stage for their successful transition to the grow-out phase.

Providing appropriate nutrition, ensuring optimal water quality, and monitoring their developmental progress are essential for promoting the healthy growth of tilapia fish fry. Consider the following key steps in fry management and growth.

7.1   Strategies for Managing Fry

Tilapia fish fry require specialized care and attention to ensure their healthy growth and development.

Implementing appropriate feeding techniques, monitoring their behavior and growth patterns, and providing a conducive rearing environment are crucial for promoting optimal fry management.

Regular observation and assessment of their nutritional requirements and growth rates can help identify any potential issues and address them promptly.

7.2   Feeding Practices for Young Tilapia Fish

Young tilapia fish have specific dietary requirements that must be met to support their rapid growth and development.

Providing a well-balanced diet, including specialized fry feed rich in essential nutrients, is essential for promoting their overall health and well-being.

Monitoring their feeding behavior and adjusting the feeding regimen as they grow can help ensure their nutritional needs are met throughout the early stages of development.

7.3   Monitoring the Growth Stages

Regular monitoring of the growth stages of tilapia fish fry is essential for assessing their overall health and development.

Tracking their growth rates, observing any physical abnormalities, and ensuring the absence of any signs of disease are critical steps in ensuring their successful transition to the grow-out phase.

Maintaining optimal water quality and providing a stress-free rearing environment are essential for promoting robust growth and development.

By implementing effective fry management strategies, providing appropriate nutrition, and closely monitoring their growth stages, you can ensure the successful development of tilapia fish fry.

In the following sections, we will explore the essential techniques for managing the pond transfer and grow-out stages of tilapia fish, laying the foundation for their successful maturation and harvest.

Chapter Eight

Pond Transfer and Grow-Out

The successful transfer of tilapia fish to ponds and their subsequent grow-out stages are crucial for their maturation and eventual harvest.

Ensuring optimal pond conditions, implementing effective feeding practices, and monitoring their overall health are essential for promoting the successful growth and development of tilapia fish.

Consider the following key steps in pond transfer and grow-out management.

8.1   Guidelines for Transferring Fish to Ponds

Transferring tilapia fish to ponds requires careful planning and consideration of various factors, including pond capacity, water quality, and stocking density.

Ensuring the acclimatization of the fish to the new environment, monitoring their behavior, and providing appropriate feed are crucial for promoting a smooth transition.

Proper handling techniques during the transfer process can help minimize stress and ensure the well-being of the fish.

8.2   Managing Tilapia Fish in the Grow-Out Stage

The grow-out stage is a critical phase in the life cycle of tilapia fish, where they reach maturity and prepare for harvest.

Providing a well-balanced diet, monitoring water quality parameters, and preventing the onset of diseases are essential for promoting their healthy growth and development.

Regular observation of their feeding behavior, growth rates, and overall health is crucial for ensuring optimal conditions for their successful maturation.

8.3   Water Quality and Feeding Management for Mature Tilapia Fish

Maintaining optimal water quality and implementing effective feeding management practices are essential for ensuring the successful maturation of tilapia fish.

Regular water testing, adjusting the feeding regimen based on their nutritional requirements, and ensuring a stress-free rearing environment are critical for promoting their overall health and well-being.

Implementing biosecurity measures to prevent disease outbreaks and monitoring their growth progress are essential for ensuring a successful harvest.

By following effective guidelines for pond transfer and implementing optimal grow-out management practices, you can ensure the successful maturation and harvest of tilapia fish.

In the following sections, we will explore the crucial aspects of disease management and prevention, as well as the essential strategies for harvesting and marketing tilapia fish, ensuring a successful aquaculture venture.

Chapter Nine

Disease Management and Prevention

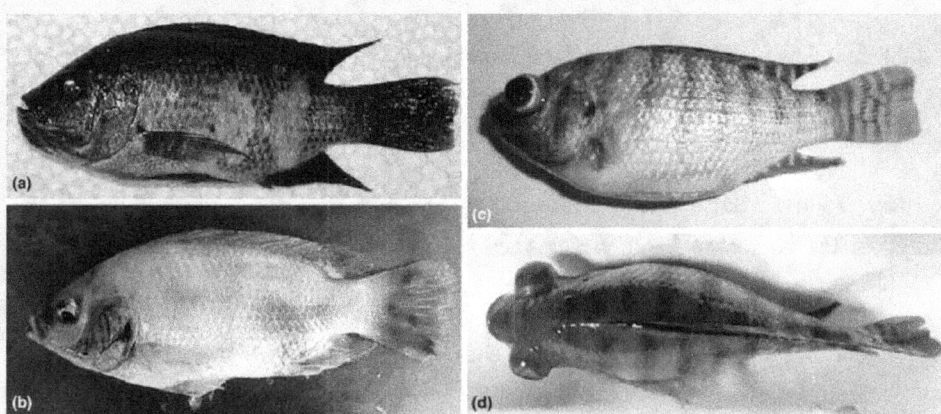

Disease management and prevention are crucial aspects of tilapia fish farming, as disease outbreaks can significantly impact the overall health and productivity of the fish.

Implementing effective biosecurity measures, practicing proper hygiene protocols, and monitoring the overall health of the fish are essential for preventing the onset of diseases.

Consider the following key steps in disease management and prevention for tilapia fish.

9.1   Common Diseases Affecting Tilapia Fish and Their Symptoms

Tilapia fish are susceptible to various diseases, including bacterial, viral, and parasitic infections, which can significantly impact their growth and survival rates.

Understanding the symptoms associated with common tilapia fish diseases, such as bacterial gill disease, streptococcosis, and tilapia lake virus (TiLV), is crucial for prompt identification and treatment.

Regular health assessments and monitoring for any signs of illness are essential for preventing disease outbreaks.

9.2 Preventative Measures for Maintaining Fish Health

Implementing effective preventative measures is crucial for maintaining the overall health and well-being of tilapia fish.

Establishing strict biosecurity protocols, maintaining optimal water quality, and ensuring a stress-free rearing environment are essential for preventing the introduction and spread of diseases.

Regular health checks, quarantine procedures for new fish introductions, and disinfection protocols for equipment and facilities can significantly reduce the risk of disease outbreaks.

9.3 Treatment Options for Common Tilapia Fish Diseases

In the event of a disease outbreak, prompt identification and implementation of appropriate treatment measures are essential for mitigating the impact on the overall fish population.

Consulting with aquatic veterinarians, implementing targeted medication regimens, and adjusting water quality parameters as necessary can help manage the spread of diseases and improve the chances of a successful recovery.

Regular monitoring of the treated fish and their environment is essential for assessing the effectiveness of the treatment and preventing any potential relapses.

By implementing effective disease management and prevention strategies, you can significantly reduce the risk of disease outbreaks and ensure the overall health and well-being of tilapia fish.

In the following sections, we will explore the essential techniques for harvesting tilapia fish and the key strategies for effectively marketing your aquaculture products, ensuring a successful venture in the aquaculture industry.

Chapter Ten

Harvesting and Marketing

The successful harvesting of tilapia fish and effective marketing strategies are crucial for realizing the benefits of your aquaculture venture.

Implementing appropriate harvesting techniques, ensuring proper storage and transportation, and developing effective marketing strategies can help maximize the profitability of your tilapia fish farming operation.

Consider the following key steps in harvesting and marketing your tilapia fish.

10.1 Techniques for Harvesting Tilapia Fish

Harvesting tilapia fish requires careful planning and consideration of various factors, including fish size, market demand, and harvest methods.

Implementing appropriate harvesting techniques, such as using specialized nets or harvesting equipment, ensures the efficient and safe collection of the fish.

Proper handling procedures and maintaining optimal water quality during the harvesting process are essential for preserving the quality and freshness of the fish.

10.2   Storage and Transportation Considerations

Proper storage and transportation are essential for preserving the quality and freshness of harvested tilapia fish.

Implementing appropriate storage techniques, such as using ice or refrigeration systems, helps maintain the fish's freshness and prevents spoilage.

Ensuring proper packaging and timely transportation to marketplaces or processing facilities are crucial for maximizing the shelf life and marketability of the fish.

10.3   Marketing Strategies for Selling Tilapia Fish

Developing effective marketing strategies is essential for promoting the sale of your tilapia fish and establishing a strong market presence.

Identifying your target market, establishing competitive pricing strategies, and creating a strong brand identity can significantly enhance the marketability of your aquaculture products.

Leveraging online platforms, participating in local markets, and establishing partnerships with distributors or retailers can help expand your customer base and increase the visibility of your tilapia fish products.

By implementing effective harvesting techniques, ensuring proper storage and transportation, and developing robust marketing strategies, you can maximize the profitability and success of your tilapia fish farming operation.

Conclusion

Congratulations! You have now gained a comprehensive understanding of the intricate process of hatching tilapia fishes.

From setting up the hatchery to managing the growth stages and ensuring the successful maturation of the fish, you have acquired valuable insights into the essential steps required for a successful tilapia fish farming venture.

By implementing the techniques and strategies outlined in this guide, you can establish a well-structured and efficient tilapia fish farming operation.

Remember to prioritize the maintenance of optimal water quality, adhere to strict biosecurity protocols, and closely monitor the health and growth of the fish throughout their life cycle.

Tilapia fish farming not only presents an opportunity for sustainable aquaculture practices but also contributes to global food security and economic development. With your newfound knowledge and expertise in hatching tilapia fishes, you are well-equipped to embark on a rewarding and successful journey in the aquaculture industry.

Best of luck in your tilapia fish farming endeavors, and may your aquaculture venture yield bountiful rewards and success!

www.ingramcontent.com/pod-product-compliance
Lightning Source LLC
Chambersburg PA
CBHW082231290526
45794CB00009B/3756